New Faculty Professional Development

✖

Planning an Ideal Program

Henryk Marcinkiewicz
& Terrence Doyle

NEW FORUMS PRESS INC.
Stillwater, Okla., U.S.A.

NEW FORUMS PRESS INC.

Published in the United States of America
by New Forums Press, Inc.1018 S. Lewis St.
Stillwater, OK 74074
www.newforums.com

Library of Congress Cataloging-in-Publication Data Pending

This book may be ordered in bulk quantities at discount from
New Forums Press, Inc., P.O. Box 876, Stillwater, OK 74076
[Federal I.D. No. 73 1123239]. Printed in the United States
of America.

International Standard Book Number: 1-58107-094-2

Contents

Chapter 1

Background, Considerations, Rationale

The Ideal Program?

We have suggested models, strategies, and tactics each of which contributes to the form of an ideal program. An ideal program would contain all of them and more. Aim for the ideal and bear in mind that it is an elusive state. This way of thinking will keep your planning dynamic and will prevent you from becoming complacent. While the entire set of suggestions would exist in an ideal program, select from among the suggestions to work with one or more of them rather than the entire set as you are organizing or refining your program. Compare what a model proposes with what is occurring at your institution. Do a gap analysis. This will identify the areas that need to be addressed as you refine and build your program. In this way you will come closer to the ideal program. Remember the goal is worth pursuing because our faculty members are directly responsible for our students' learning.

What is this book about?

This book is about organizing and conducting a development program for new faculty for an entire year. The length of time for the program is a significant departure from current practice at all but a few institutions. Typical professional development programs for new faculty are orientations around the start of a school year and last from one day to one week. Some institutions conduct semester-long programs. An entire academic year is recommended for a number of reasons.

First, an academic year is the elemental scheduling unit for a complete cycle in academe. Aligning the development program with the cycle of the academic calendar supports the integration of professional development into an institution. When continual professional development activities coincide with the academic calendar, the lessons learned can also be used continuously and as they occur rather than sporadically; there is greater proximity between what is being learned and the opportunity to try what is being learned in the classroom. When professional development is a part of the regular calendar, there is more opportunity for using what one learns.

Secondly, learning takes time, especially considering that the largest portion of learning involves the opportunity to practice. New faculty need time to try out some of the ideas that are new to them.

Finally, besides learning about teaching and learning, there is the learning associated with socialization and making the transition to the new environment and the new job that are fundamental to new faculty and which take time. A full year gives new faculty enough time to lay the foundation for their professional development as well as for the acclimatization to their new lives.

Philosophy

The first year of a faculty member's life at a university should not be a "trial by fire," but rather, it is an acknowledgment of the needs that professionals have when they enter into a new academic institution. New faculty deserve an orientation to their new institution, the profession, the academic community, and the social community and the expectations that each of these entities have upon an individual. Faculty members learn throughout their orientation and important questions and issues emerge related to their work and their socialization that could not have occurred to them at the beginning of a school year. A new faculty program is best organized as a year long effort to allow the time to address the variety of expectations.

New Faculty? Incoming Faculty? Who are you working with?

Some of the individuals who are newly-hired at your institution are new to teaching, others are not but instead do have teaching experience. It would be accurate to refer to the latter group as incoming faculty but not necessarily as "new" faculty: they are new to your institution but not teaching. Inexperienced faculty members are both new to teaching and to your institution. (Except that it does happen that an institution will hire its own graduates to teach who therefore they are not new to the institution. Or, occasionally professors will return to an institution after a departure.) There are not compelling reasons to exclude experienced, incoming faculty from participating in professional development together with their inexperienced colleagues. On the contrary, it is recommended that all incoming faculty experience an introductory professional development and transition program together—they will learn from each other, get to know each other, and grow as a cohort. For this reason and to simplify the reference

3

to both groups, together they will be referred to as "new" faculty throughout this book. "New" faculty also reflects the popular term used for both groups.

Who is this book for?

This book is for administrators, faculty, and other staff who are involved with the professional development of faculty. In particular, this book will be useful to individuals working with new faculty.

Purpose

This book offers suggestions and rationales for organizing, conducting, and maintaining a long-term program for new faculty. Such a program will at once aid in orientation, transition, and professional development.

Who is this program for?

This program is for all new faculty members who are incoming employees some of whom have never taught and whose experience in teaching and learning is limited to their time as students. Some new faculty are experienced and will have taught for a number of years. The professional preparation of the new faculty will vary according to the needs and practices of your institution. Some will hold traditional degrees others will hold highly-specialized certificates or licenses and still others may hold a combination of credentials. Most will be highly intelligent and have special skills. Most all will be new to your new institution. They share a common calling though they differ by their fields of study. They share a common lack of familiarity with their new professional home. They vary in their degree of experience in working and in working as educators. They vary in their familiarity with students in general but they share a lack of familiarity with your students in particular. They share a common motivation and appreciation for teaching and learning. They vary in their professional preparation in education. Very significantly, they have succeeded in your hiring process and you have succeeded in attracting them to your institution!

Why Emphasize Teaching and Learning?

The basic reason is straightforward: teachers in higher education need professional development because few are ever prepared to be teachers. Add to that, that teaching is a difficult job requiring knowledge of planning, people, practices, psychology and expertise in a subject area. Besides, the characteristics of college students' change and so even veteran teachers benefit from learning about teaching and learning. Finally, our knowledge about how to teach effectively is improving and changing. This last reason is based on twelve facts about teaching and learning.

1. The availability of information and the ways it can be used by the learner varies by the ways, context, complexity, challenge and transfer of the information being taught (Zull, 2002). This presents a double challenge, first in considering that most of the professoriate has never had any formal training in how to teach. Second, these expectations challenge traditional views of the role of a teacher as the source of knowledge and learning rather than as the orchestrator of learning experiences.

2. Until recently, there has been little scientific understanding of the relationship between how the brain

works and learning. Teaching practices were probably closer to folklore than to scientific knowledge (Sylwester, 1995). New understanding of the role of the brain's development influences teaching.

3. The learners' prior experiences play the single biggest role in their learning but the teacher has no control over them. (Ausubel, 1968).

4. Emotion is woven into every aspect of the learning process but teachers have only limited control of the emotions involved in learning (Zull, 2002; Atkinson & Shiffrin, 1968).

5. Helping learners to unlearn behaviors, concepts, ideas etc. that are mistaken is more difficult, but necessary, than teaching them new learning (Starbuck, 1996).

6. Teachers have very little time to teach learners compared to the time learners have on their own. The average 3 credit college class (45 hours per semester—three hours per week) equals only .017% of a week.

7. Most learning occurs outside the classroom. When a learner is exposed to a new pattern of signals from the outside world—a teacher for example—the strengths of the synaptic contacts and local biochemical and electrical properties gradually change in complex distributed constellations. This represents learning as we understand it today (Goldberg, 2001). This process takes time—time to reflect, practice, apply, and test out the new patterns. The extent to which each student spends the necessary time for learning to occur is not under the direct control of the teacher.

8. The range of the learners' abilities from low to high that is often present in any given classroom makes providing learning opportunities simultaneously and

equally to all of the students difficult and in some cases simply not possible to do.

9. We learn through practice, the manipulation of information, whether through physical movement or intellectual questioning.

10. We learn when the target of learning is within proximity: it is close at hand, in representation, or in imagination.

11. The brain's ability to visualize is arguably the most significant aspect of cognition. The visual world is literally mapped in our brains. Teachers need to understand the power of using images to teach (Kossyln, 1996).

12. Emotion permeates every aspect of learning. Fear, control and pleasure play significant roles in students' learning (LeDoux, 2001)

The implications of the above considerations for teaching are compelling enough to require new faculty to continuously learn about teaching and learning. Additionally, there are other major factors affecting higher education that underscore the need for new faculty professional development.

Demographic Changes

There are more differences among students now than there have ever been. There are more non-traditional students, there are more students from groups that had previously been unrepresented, and there are more students overall. In fact, nearly 70% of all high school graduates now attempt college in some form. Within the new, more diverse student body is one significant distinction—it is the number of under-prepared students entering college who need the guidance and skill of effective teachers if they are to succeed.

Robert Sylwester writing on the application of findings from neuroscience to teaching and learning summarizes a dilemma of teaching, "Deep down, we could never be sure if students learned because of our efforts or despite them" (1995). This observation was true at the beginning of the 20th century too when most college students were high achievers, the best and the brightest— and wealthiest and the prevailing format for instruction was teacher-centered with students being responsible for their own learning. Most students would teach themselves, organizing information that was not clear, disciplining themselves to do their out-of-class work and generally overcoming any "teaching barriers" that the professor would put in their way. Today our colleges and universities are filled with a completely different population of students. Levine and Cureton in *When Hope and Fear Collide*, suggest "The education we offered to previous generations, whether successful or not, will not work with these students. They are different and their times are different" (1999).

The percentage of high school graduates aged 16–24 enrolled in college rose from 46.6% in 1973 to 65.0% in 1996 and continues to rise. The proportion of college students 25 and older increased from 28% in 1970 to 44% in 1995. (*AAHE-Bulletin*, 1998).

The proportion of high school sophomores whose teachers, counselors, and parents encouraged them to go to college increased dramatically between 1980 and 1990. In 1990, more than half of even the lowest performing sophomores (those scoring in the lowest quartile on mathematics and reading tests) were advised to attend college.

These statistics underscore the point that students enrolling in various colleges and universities are more diverse, less prepared to be independent learners, and need teacher-directed guidance in their learning, if they are to be successful, more than ever before (Levine & Cureton, 1999). The consequential demands on the professoriate are that it must be prepared, first of all. Second, its preparation must be different than whatever had been done to prepare professors previously. Colleges and universities must help develop the teaching skills of their professors; otherwise, the needs of students will not be met.

Today's college students are different. There are more older students in college than ever. They are insufficiently prepared for academic work, yet their confidence in their abilities is higher than ever! These latter factors are likely foremost on the minds of faculty members when they insist that today's generation is a different breed. One characterization between students nowadays and former generations is that the differences are cultural more than academic. Acknowledging the generational differences will serve as a first step in determining the types of relationships we need to establish with our students of tomorrow (*AAHE Bulletin,* 1998).

The Rate at which New Information Changes the Role of Teachers

Nobel laureate Herbert Simon made the pivotal observation that the meaning of knowing has shifted from being able to remember and repeat information to being able to find and use it" (1996). "As a result of the accumulation of new kinds of information about human learning, views of how effective learning proceeds have shifted from the benefits of diligent drill and practice to focus on students' understanding and application of knowledge. The goal of education is...helping students develop the intellectual tools and learning strategies needed to acquire the knowledge necessary to think productively." (Bransford, Brown, & Cocking, 1999).

This shift in view about what it means to know creates practical challenges for the professoriate. A teaching challenge before the shift would have been to decide which content to teach from all the content possible in a subject. A new challenge expands the earlier one; not only must the professor select the most important content, but in addition the professor must teach students the learning strategies and intellectual tools they need. Where does a professor learn to do this if faculty members are hired as content experts?

A related concern is the effect of the sheer increase in information. Daniel Boorstin (1995) suggests that the 500 years ago there was little information but much meaning, while today the reverse is true: there is much information and little meaning or understanding of it all. The mass of information makes it nearly impossible for one to remain an expert in the traditional sense as one who has mastery of knowledge in an area. There is just too much for one person to be a complete expert in the same way. This change must affect the way that faculty need to function professionally. What Simon and Bransford, Brown, and Cocking suggest about our students is also true for faculty. They can no longer have the same aspiration for knowing it all, but rather have to learn to have the knowledge to think productively.

Faculty clearly need assistance in coming to terms with these questions and the role changes brought about by the ever increasing growth of knowledge. Education today is not only the giving of information but it is preparing students to live lives that they have not yet experienced.

Biology and Teaching

A colleague once remarked that his father who was a professor of education for thirty-five years knew it was time to retire when the newest ideas being passed around about teaching and learning were in essence the same ideas he had already seen three times before. With the current developments in neuroscience research, the old professor would likely still be teaching because teaching and learning have entered a new frontier of information to consider. For the first time, we have a functional understanding of the brain in respect of learning. The new insights to the brain have brought about a clearer understanding of how learning occurs. James Zull (2002) suggests that, "Ultimately, we will still have to reconcile everything with nature. If we find our theories about teaching to be in disagreement with biology, we must reconsider them."

Whether it is new understanding of how neurons "fire and wire together," or what causes them to stay together or break apart, or the role emotion plays in learning or how memories are constructed a new biologically driven frontier of teaching and learning is opening. While this new research has not been formalized enough to prescribe teaching approaches, it does begin to shape the designs of effective learning environments (Zull, 2002). New faculty need to know about this new and exciting research and its implications and how to use it to build approaches that will increase learning and student success.

The Changing Professoriate

Periodically, there are opportunities to make significant changes in the way that colleges and universities conduct themselves. Such an opportunity now avails itself as large numbers of veteran faculty members are retiring making way for equally large numbers of new faculty. This phenomenon is changing the membership of the professoriate in American colleges and universities. The opportunity in these large scale personnel changes is in implementing a systematic and commonly shared approach to faculty professional development. An institution with a professional development program for new faculty can ensure that at a minimum, all of the new faculty will have had the opportunity to be exposed to a common set of topics about teaching and learning.

A benefit of this shared experience is that it helps build esprit de corps and facilitates communication among the faculty because there are common terms and experiences. The shared experience of participating in professional develpoment also adds definition to the institutional culture.

Enhancing Higher Education as a Profession

Virtually all professions in the United States require continuing education to maintain an individual's status as a professional. This is not true for the teaching portion of a professor's job. Simply, for the professoriate there is no professional requirement to continue learning in order to maintain one's status. In spite of this, a few institutions impose such requirements on their faculty and indeed it is likely generally true that professors continue learning independently due to the nature of the learning profession. If a professional consensus existed, it would serve to guide the profession. The lack of such a professional consensus creates an opportunity for institutions to assume the role of caretakers and guides for the professional development of their faculty members.

Better Teaching Improves Student Learning

If we had no faith in the effects of teaching, we would not teach. Perhaps we teach in response to the human need to learn as Senge suggests that we communicate to learn something (1990). Teaching as a human endeavor varies by degrees of effectiveness of orchestrating the experience in which an individual learns—there is excellent teaching and poor teaching.

The term "improving students' learning" was entered into an online search engine to estimate the number of sites that would be related. There were over 1,200,000 sites nominally related to the term. A cursory review of some 1,000 sites revealed three areas. First, there was the use of technology as an instructional tool. Second, there was the better preparation of teachers to use proven methods and approaches to teaching. Third, there was the giving of emotional and social support to learners. The volume of these results suggests that the improvement of learning by the improvement of teaching is a popular notion. The previously referenced question of whether students learn because of us or in-spite of us should now be answered with a resounding, "Because of us," if we develop faculty who are skilled teachers.

New Faculty Find it Enjoyable and Helpful

The professional development of new faculty and the entire academic community must be engaged in learning-to-learn. The comments of University of Cincinnati President Joseph A. Steger, and Lanthan D. Camblin Jr., associate professor of education simultaneously summarize the need for faculty development and set the stage for that very activity, "Where do we find the faculty who can accept this challenge? I have said all along that we will find them on our campuses today. Our faculty know the challenge. They need only the resources to respond and to succeed in the new role that is demanded of them."

References

Atkinson, R.C., & Shiffrin, R.M. (1968). Human memory: A proposed system and its control processes. In K. W. Spence & J. T. Spence (Eds.), *Psychology of learning and motivation* (Vol. 2). New York: Academic Press.

Ausubel, D.P. (1968). *Educational psychology: A cognitive view.* New York: Holt, Rinehart and Winston.

Boorstin, D.J. (1995). *Cleopatra's nose: Essays on the unexpected.* New York: Vintage.

Bransford, J. D., Brown, A. L., & Cocking, R. R. (1999). *How people learn: Brain, mind, experience, and school.* Washington, DC: National Academy Press. pp.xi [Available online at http://www.nap.edu/html/howpeople1/].

Goldberg, E. (2001). *The executive brain, frontal lobes and the civilized mind.* New York: Oxford University Press.

Kossyln, A. (1996). *Images and the brain.* Cambridge, MA: MIT Press.

LeDoux, J. (2001). *The emotional brain.* New York: Simon & Schuster.

Levine, A. & Cureton, J.S. (1999). *When hope and fear collide: A portrait of today's college student.* San Francisco: Jossey-Bass.

Marcinkiewicz, H. R., & Sylwester, R. (November/December, 2003). The brain, technology, and education: An interview with

Robert Sylwester. *The Technology Source* [http://ts.mivu.org]

Senge, P. (1990). *The fifth discipline.* New York: Currency Doubleday

Simon, H. (1996). *Observations on the sciences of science learning.* Paper presented at Carnegie Mellon University.

Starbuck, W.H. (1996). Unlearning ineffective or obsolete technologies. *International Journal of Technology Management, 11*: 725–737.

Sylwester, R. (1995). *A celebration of neurons: An educator's guide to the human brain.* Chicago: Zephyr Press.

Teaching Ideas #8: Essential demographics of today's college students. (November, 1998). *AAHE-Bulletin, 51*(3).

Zull, J. (2002). *The art of changing the brain.* Sterling, VA: Stylus

What are the Goals of an Extended Development and Transition Program for New Faculty?

Improving student learning

There are a number of goals for an extended program for new faculty, however, the overarching goal should parallel the predominant one of institutions of higher learning—the improvement of student learning. The relationship of teaching to this goal is elemental; yet, most new faculty enter the professoriate without formal preparation for teaching; therefore there need to be opportunities for faculty to get preparation for teaching so that they can contribute more effectively to student learning. Colleges and universities ought to provide these opportunities to new faculty otherwise the institutions will have to do without the benefit of trained and prepared new faculty. Alternatively, they may be forced to assume the strategy of hoping to attract prepared professors from other institutions. One reason for the lack of preparation for teaching among new faculty is that there is not a national consensus for the preparation of professors as might be expected by a certifying agency. Neither is there a professional mandate for preparation in teaching at the college level as there is at the elementary and secondary levels. It is fundamental to the support of an institution's mission that new faculty be prepared for teaching. When the faculty teach better, students learn better.

Faculty will acquire and improve their teaching skills as they continue to learn. Establish the expectations that teaching and learning are important. Promote a common vocabulary about teaching and learning. Faculty learning should become the institutional norm.

Demonstrating the importance teaching has for the institution

"Teaching in colleges is marked by historic paradox: though institutions constantly talk up its importance, they evaluate faculty primarily on the basis of scholarly achievements outside the classroom" (Seldin, 1995). One way for an institution to make a public demonstration of its commitment to teaching is by establishing an extended development program for new faculty with a strong emphasis on helping faculty to become better teachers. Seldin suggests that the new emphasis on teaching results from a combination of forces social, political, technological, and demographic as well as the ongoing demands for accountability in education. Colleges and universities have come under increasing pressure from students, parents and legislatures to improve the quality of their teaching. Institutions can begin this process with their "new" employees and publicly demonstrate their commitment to improving teaching.

Facilitating faculty integration into the communities both academic and local

Successfully moving into a new community and assuming a new job requires assistance. This is another goal of an extended professional development program—to assist new faculty with making the transition into their new situations. The pressure to get ready for the first semester of classes, committee work, and research is greatly reduced if new faculty have the benefit of assistance in coping with the issues related to their new home lives. These can range from finding housing to finding day care to interlibrary loan policies, all of which are made easier by an extended transition program. Often new faculty do not even know what their "important" questions are, they evolve such as when the day comes that they need to get library cards for the public library or need to find a dentist, dry cleaner or a babysitter, to name just a few of the services for which they may need referral.

Five years of evaluations from the year-long program at Ferris State (2003) revealed that among the most valued aspects of the program was the opportunity to get questions answered in a safe and comfortable environment as they occurred throughout the academic year. Faculty indicated that having a reliable resource person from the Center for Teaching, Learning and Faculty Development was a key to making their transition smoother and less stressful. In addition, the faculty indicated that being able to build connections with colleagues from across campus and sharing in discussions about teaching and students' learning problems made their efforts to participate very worthwhile. Many new faculty were simply unaware that their colleagues were having similar experiences in and out of the classroom and were greatly relieved to find that they were not alone in their experiences and also that there were empathetic colleagues with whom to commiserate or congratulate.

The "trial by fire" model of orientation to higher education in which a new professor is left to one's own devices does not result in the outcome that the strongest can survive, but rather it results in causing colleges and universities to lose people who could have made awesome contributions to their academic communities had they been given reasonable assistance with their transition. Including transition assistance as a part of professional development can improve the retention of new faculty and save hiring costs in the process. Ferris State University found that the average position search cost several thousands of dollars when expenses and search committee time were considered. A supportive faculty transition program can save an institution money.

Promoting a culture of continuous learning among faculty

The old saw that you only get one chance to make a first impression has bearing for new faculty as well. Institutions that offer faculty an extended program geared to meeting both their personal transition needs and their professional ones increase the likelihood that the faculty will be lifelong users of professional development services. An extended program showcases faculty development services, demonstrates to new faculty the value and commitment the institution places on continuous learning and establishes relationships with faculty that can last a career. An additional finding from the Ferris State University program was that faculty saw the program as a commitment on the part of the institution to faculty, to teaching and to valuing them personally as new members of the academic community.

New faculty making new friends

Much current literature on teaching and learning emphasizes the importance of building connections and community with students and offering them more control of their own learning as a means of creating a positive and stimulating learning environment. (See for examples: Weimer, 2002; Bransford, Brown, & Cocking, 1999; Rogers, 1999; Kuh, Schuh, & Whitt, 1991). This is true for faculty as well. One of the most positive outcomes from an extended transition program is the bonding and relationships that are formed among faculty from all disciplines of a college or university. There are not only professional relationships formed where research projects are planned or grant ideas are formulated but personal friendships where faculty discover others with similar personal and social interests such as the Boy Scouts, playing golf, tennis, or jogging, or worshipping the same faith, or having young children looking for play mates. The relationships formed through the transition emphasis of a development programs helps new faculty make the transition to a new environment less stressfully and fosters a positive view of the institution and its faculty development center.

References

Bransford, J. D., Brown, A. L., & Cocking, R. R. (1999). *How people learn: Brain, mind, experience, and school.* Washington, DC: National Academy Press. [Available online at http://www.nap.edu/html/howpeople1/].

Doyle, T. (2003) *Summary of the First Five Years of the New to Ferris Faculty Transition program.* Big Rapids, MI: Ferris State University.

Kuh, G. D., Schuh, J.S., Whitt, E.J., & Associates (1991). *Involving colleges: Successful approaches to fostering student learning and personal development outside the classroom.* San Francisco: Jossey-Bass.

Rogers, S. (1999). *Motivation & learning, the high performance toolbox and teaching tips.* Evergreen, CO: Peak Learning Systems.

Seldin, P. & Associates, (1995). *Improving college teaching.* Bolton, MA: Anker.

Weimer, M. (2002). *Learner-centered teaching 2002.* San Francisco: Jossey-Bass.

Chapter 3

Implementing a program: What needs to be considered?

There are many considerations in organizing a new faculty program, but there is some comfort in knowing that the considerations are not infinite and therefore manageable. Thomas Gilbert suggested a set of conditions for promoting competence (1978). The model is useful because it organizes the necessary conditions into distinct categories and it is intuitively-appealing. A goal of the model, competence, is a worthwhile one to strive for, though it might not be the most obvious one when planning for new faculty partly because we expect them to be highly-educated or highly-experienced or both and so we might think of them as being competent not only in their respective fields but also as teachers. What we want to promote for our new faculty is competence in teaching and in functioning at the institution.

Model of Competence

There are three conditions that must be satisfied in order to enable competence in general and for our purposes, competence in teaching. There are two contributing "partners." One is the environment, which in this case is the academic institution. The other partner is the new faculty member. The involvement or participation of both partners is essential in order to satisfy all three conditions. The contribution of the partners for each of the conditions can be illustrated in a matrix. Note that the partners' effects are complementary.

Motivation and Incentives—What Works?

INTERNAL personal	Motivation	Understanding and agreement	Capacity, capability and inclination
EXTERNAL institutional	Incentive	Information and expectations	Equipment and strategies

Making a distinction between external incentives from internal motivation is useful for operational purposes. In this book, incentives refer to the contributions of the institution and motivation refers to the participatory drive of the individual faculty member. At the same time, we should not lose sight of the integral relationship of the two. The image of water nourishing a plant exemplifies the co-dependent nature of incentives and motivation. Even the idea of plants in general is an appropriate metaphor for motivation since some plants require more or less water, or more or less incentive. Those requiring less could be thought of as being more internally-motivated or less-dependent on external incentives.

Appropriate questions to pursue in organizing your new faculty development program include, "What incentives are meaningful to faculty?" and "What incentives does the institution provide?"

An incentive will not be effective if it holds no appeal for an individual. This is also true of new faculty participating in a development program. We have found from the responses of faculty we have worked with that one of the most effective incentives was the ac-knowledgment of the faculty as professionals—they were given respect. Money, time off, and more tangible rewards were considered less important and even less desirable unless they supported the aspect of respecting faculty as professionals.

Novelty. The circumstance of newly-hired faculty has a special characteristic—novelty—in that there are new employees entering a new situation. Several incentives may be having an effect including the desire on the part of the new employee to do well: this is a self-imposed incentive or an internal motivation. Some institutions may require that new faculty participate in a program: authority is the incentive, compliance is the motivation.

Camaraderie. This is a compelling incentive. Sometimes to the dismay of the faculty development office, the participants will thank you or highlight on their evaluations of sessions that what they enjoyed most was the opportunity to meet and socialize with their colleagues. This incentive seems to underlie most all of the activities that are done and does not necessarily mean that the topics were not appreciated. It does, however, illustrate powerfully the need and appreciation for human contact within our profession and the strength of collegiality as an incentive. Knowing that faculty respond well to situations in which their colleagues are participating motivates them; therefore, use group meetings as an incentive whether it is having groups as participants or groups of faculty conducting panel sessions. Faculty members also seem to learn well from each other. You might say it is an example of the "bright leading the bright."

Opportunity to learn. This is an incentive that

serves the nature of faculty. After all, most of us enter the professoriate because of our love of learning. Providing opportunities to learn makes sense for us. To use this as an incentive, remind faculty that they will be learning something new or confirming something already known. Remind them of the advantage of being in the learner's "chair" to recall what it is like to be at the "receiving" end.

Sustaining motivation. In most instances new faculty will be motivated to participate in a program for them. A challenge may emerge later on in sustaining motivation to participate for the long term as in a year long program. There might be competing incentives from other parts of the institution enticing the faculty not to participate. For example, the demands of the job may occupy a professor's time more than he or she can manage. Parts of the institution may override schedules of your program such as when there are department meetings and the professor must choose between attending the program and the meeting; or, the Human Resources department is conducting a mandatory workshop on prevention of sexual harassment during your program time. Some of the countering incentives are logistical and can be prevented if you plan well ahead and have the commitment from the various parts of the institution to keep the new faculty program time free for their participation. Advise senior management to schedule days throughout the year for professional development or institutional business. This is not an uncommon practice and helps many areas within an institution.

At the same time, the institution needs to plan the logistics to allow new faculty to participate in their program. Logistical obstacles to participation include scheduling the new professor with an overload of courses or all different courses or, otherwise requiring him or her to pay inordinate attention to preparation for classes. Advise the Deans' Council about the benefits of not overloading new faculty.

Group expectations. Incentives come not only from within the institution, but they also could come from the students, professional organizations, and colleagues. In predicting the integration of technology in instruction, it was found that the best predictor was whether faculty felt that they were expected to integrate technology into teaching by the four groups mentioned (Marcinkiewicz & Regstad, 1996). Faculty were motivated by their perception; the incentive—subjective norms—was the expressed expectation for faculty to use technology in teaching. The incentive was akin to peer pressure.

To sustain the motivation to participate in professional development beyond the incentives of contractual obligations, love of learning, camaraderie, and a reasonable work schedule, etc. you would do well to organize activities that have the following characteristics. They are attention-getting, basically there is an interest. They are relevant. They inspire the new professor's confidence, and they provide the new professor with satisfaction. These characteristics are eponymous for the ARCS model of motivation which summarizes major findings about motivation (Keller, 1987).

It is somewhat elusive to separate an incentive from the act of being motivated. Incentives have characteristics, are provided by someone, and in the case of subjective norms or other internal motivation are internal incentives. The result of being motivated is that a person pursues an action, or sustains it, or is energized towards it. The consideration for running new faculty development programs is that we need to understand the faculty, identify the kinds of incentives that would motivate them, and provide them institutionally.

Equipment and Capacity

The availability of appropriate equipment as well as the capacity, inclination, or the learned ability to use the equipment is another condition needed for competence. First, let's look at the equipment that the institution would provide. Consider equipment in the broadest sense. It includes machinery, computers, and other devices, but it also includes software, planning and strategic models and other tools useful for doing the work of teaching and learning. The institution needs to help assess the needs of the new faculty and provide appropriate instruction.

What the new faculty are responsible for is the capacity and ability to learn as well as the actual learning. Not everyone has the same degree of inclination towards, desire, nor the ability to use certain equipment. Whether new faculty meet this condition helps you determine the need for training. If new faculty come unequipped with the skills and abilities to use the hardware, software, and strategic thinking of teaching, they need to learn them from their professional development program.

Information and Understanding

What must happen with information? What is the nature of information? The institution must have a clear mission, vision, or other guiding purpose. There must be an effective system of communication. The institution's messages about its expectations must be continuously and variously delivered whether by using multiple formats or by multiple schedules of presentation in order to increase the likelihood of being attended to, understood, and hopefully agreed with. The messages must be consistent with the mission. They must be communicated to all personnel.

It is essential that the information be based on the expectations that the institution has for its faculty members, that the expectations be communicated, and that the faculty receive and understand the expectations.

The faculty must participate in the communication system. They must receive the communication. They must understand what is communicated. They must accept what is communicated. They must act upon the expectations of them.

Logistics

Time-scheduling: Faculty members work a variety of schedules; therefore, the schedules for their professional development activities must be varied. The best advice for scheduling for current faculty is to offer a variety of schedules, venues, and repeated sessions. However, for the new faculty, it would be desirable to gather all members simultaneously. This is the goal and it can be achieved if your institution designates times during the month that are dedicated to faculty professional development.

Costs

The major expense for a new faculty professional development program is that of the personnel managing it. Other typical expenses include instructional materials, refreshments, and occasional stipend money either for other faculty members to participate in training sessions as panel members or for other facilitators.

Collective Bargaining Units

Will all new faculty participate? Will this be a requirement? Who will enforce it? Will it be a problem for your union? These are questions to consider if your faculty members are organized in a collective bargaining unit. It is interesting that if new faculty are required to participate in professional development as a condition of their employment, then contriving incentives is still necessary to sustain their interest and participation. Required participation does help you because it simplifies planning.

References

Gilbert, T. F. (1978). *Human competence: Engineering worthy performance.* New York: McGraw Book Company.

Keller, J. M. (1987). Development and use of the ARCS model of motivational design. *Journal of Instructional Development, 10*(3), 2-10.

Marcinkiewicz, H. R., Regstad, N. G. (1996). Using subjective norms to predict teachers' computer use. *Journal of Computing in Teacher Education, 13*(1), 27–33

Chapter 4

Planning instruction for faculty: What are the objectives?

The primary objective ought to be the improved learning of students—the students of the new faculty members', that is. Some other objectives that are less general but still contribute to the primary one include instruction about:
- the professoriate;
- instructional development; and
- support of the institution.

The objectives for particular training sessions will of course need to reflect the topic and the level of understanding or proficiency of the new faculty. It is important to remember in planning for new faculty development that you are preparing instruction and that new faculty are learners. Just like other learners, their learning takes time. In other words, do not expect understanding, proficiency, or integration in practice of a subject taught just because a new faculty member has been introduced to it once. Instruction deserves repetition, especially in the practice phase of it, if not in the presentation phase of it.

If you plan as for instruction and you have a good idea of your objectives, you need to consider the same factors that you would consider in planning instruction for any learners. The four factors affecting learning suggested by Bransford (1979) are the basis for most of your instructional planning concerns. They are an understanding of the learners' characteristics, media, methods, and assessment.

Learners' Characteristics — of the New Faculty

How will the characteristics of the new faculty influence their instruction?

A starting point for planning is to appraise the group of learners—the new faculty—for the characteristics that may influence how they learn and to plan the most effective use of media and methods.

Love of learning. First of all, consider that most people who work in higher education do so to teach. Even most administrators start from faculty positions. Individuals enter teaching often because of their love of learning. An excellent summary of that was expressed by a professor once during an interview for hiring..."…this is the best possible job anyone can have. You learn constantly to keep ahead and you actually get paid for it. It's great…" Faculty members are in their jobs largely because of their love for learning. Add to that the possibility to share with others what you love—though the "others" are most often the students who may not share the same enthusiasm—and you are identifying traits that are characteristic of teaching and continuing scholarship.

Intelligence and collegiality. Of course, professors expect to learn so that they may develop a level of expertise because all faculty are expected to be experts in their areas of specialization. To aspire and to achieve a level of expertise requires high intelligence and persistence. A consequence of pursuing expertise in an area can be and sometimes needs to be narrow and may be sparsely populated. That is to say that faculty members either start out with or end up with a measure of individualism. At the same time, faculty members staunchly defend and support their colleagues in the professoriate against those from without: they protect the group of individuals.

Novelty. In addition to many of the traits described, new faculty members have additional traits related to the novelty of their situation. They may be novices to the profession, and most of the new faculty would be newcomers to your institution as well. So, there are professional and social aspects of the uninitiated that need to be considered.

Promotion. When you compare the opportunities for promotion within the professoriate with a corporate employment or other sectors where an individual with a professor's expertise may work, it emerges that the opportunities are outweighed in favor of the corporate sector. Simply, there are few steps for promotion for professors even though they are steep and slow to climb. Not all of the faculty pursue promotion, though most are required to pursue tenure or a status akin to tenure. Because a professor has limited opportunity for advancement, professional satisfaction—and its parent, motivation—resides in other activities: teaching, writing, research, organizational involvement, etc. This aspect of the professoriate influences the incentives that appeal to the faculty.

Practicality. Even though your new faculty members are bright and well-educated, there is a distinct preference in their professional development for emphasizing the practical aspect of teaching and learning and not emphasizing the theoretical. This does not mean that they do not have an appreciation for theory. On the contrary, they will better appreciate the practical suggestions, models, strategies, etc. if they do have a basis in theory that has been supported by research and practice.

From these simple characterizations, we can draw a few traits that may be useful in planning instruction for new faculty. New faculty love to learn, are intelligent, are individualistic, support their colleagues, may be new to the profession, will not be socialized to the institution, are not on a "fast track" to promotion, and appreciate practical suggestions.

Characterizing your students, the new faculty, is the first step in planning your instruction. Keep in mind that your characterization—the identification of traits that affect their learning—can be more specific than what has been described. For example, you may be working with a target group of professors all within the same field of study, and for all of whom English is their second language. These additional traits may influence your further instructional planning.

Media—What media work best with new faculty?

Faculty members enjoy working with their colleagues. They learn well from each other. This can be attributed to the strong sense of support among the professoriate. In acknowledgment of this trait, an appropriate selection for the use of media is the human voice of faculty peers in the form of panel or individual peer presentations.

If you are training new faculty in the use of hardware or software, use the actual equipment. One of the traits that support this choice of medium is the new faculty members' novelty with the subject being taught. This choice follows from Bruner's (1964) suggested preference for cognitive representation, an important point of which is that an enactive medium (hands on) is appropriate when a subject is new to learners. This recommendation also comes from the feedback we have collected in working with new faculty. Refer to Appendix A for a list of types of media.

Methods — What methods work best with new faculty?

Even if the new faculty are required to participate in professional development their schedules will likely be crowded. Bear in mind that they will need to be making practical arrangements to establish themselves in the community in addition to preparing for teaching and in addition to acculturating themselves to the institution's system of practices. The methods you employ will need to be useable during short periods of time, and sometimes over the course of an irregular schedule. They need to be efficient and effective of themselves since it may not be possible for the new faculty member to predictably schedule review or study time.

An alternative to self-contained lessons is for new faculty to practice the points taught during the course of their classes. One way to orchestrate this approach is for the faculty to try one point, inform the students that their intent is to practice a teaching point, get the students continuing feedback on that point, and report to the group of new faculty on their experience.

If you are training for equipment or software be patient and organize your sessions so that there are many opportunities for individual attention. New faculty do not have much time to spend on professional development and so the available time should be spent efficiently. Add to that the fact that they are intelligent and scholars in some area but may be uncomfortable when they are in the unfamiliar pose of not being expert with a computer or software. It takes courage to admit to being a novice or rank beginner one minute while most of the work day you are expected to be an expert. So, be patient with your new faculty. Do not draw on their supply of courage interminably. Provide enough instructors so that the instructor-to-learner ratios are low so that each professor may be afforded individual attention.

For teaching about teaching and learning, keep the instruction direct by showing the practical applications and minimizing theory. New faculty appreciate knowing that what they are learning is supported by theory, or research and practice but they do not necessarily benefit from nor want to have a mastery of the theories themselves.

If you are using the voices and bodies of faculty colleagues as your media, then include combinations of those human resources. Use presentations by panels or individuals. For these presentations veteran faculty members are appropriate. Use discussion groups, lectures and other methods that are human-voice based.

The choice of these methods is supported by the characteristic of faculty that they enjoy learning and do well learning from each other. Oftentimes, they are also the sole experts on a topic as in when they share experiences unique to being a new faculty member. After all, one can only be a new faculty member at the same institution once.

Finally, practice "learner-centered faculty development" and apply two key principles: provide the opportunity to practice during instruction what is being taught and tailor the instruction to fit the needs of the learner. Refer to Appendix B: Methods.

Assessment — How will you assess the learning of new faculty?

Assessing learning helps you to know whether or not your efforts have been effective. So, what kind of assessment is most appropriate to be done? Recall, that if you start from the premise that conducting professional development activities for new faculty is akin to planning instruction, then you have the advantage of a basis for assessment—the objectives. The overall objective is improved student learning. Getting data for progress towards this objective does take awhile and it is hard to discriminate the specific effect of faculty professional development because there are so many variables involved in student learning. Still, it is possible to suggest an effect but data would need to be collected for a year or longer.

A form of assessment or evaluation should be included at the time that objectives are identified. This is important advice because you need to avoid incongruence between the objectives and the assessment. This is the mismatch that occurs as when, for example the objective of instruction may be the successful writing of a course syllabus, but the assessment of a new faculty member's learning of that may include the history of an institution. The point is that objectives and assessments should match and that identifying both simultaneously prevents mismatch or incongruence.

A useful assessment device is the Small Group Instructional Diagnosis (Clark & Redmond, 1982). Simply, it is a 3-question set to which groups of individuals respond and discuss their responses until there is a consensus to their responses. The groups' responses are then prioritized. This process may suffice as feedback for the professional development sessions for new faculty. This tool is primarily used for getting feedback from students at the early part of a semester, but is also appropriate to use for assessing your instruction.

It is often informative to solicit anecdotal responses from participants as well.

Data Base

If you are beginning a new faculty development program, begin a database of participation in activities by the faculty. Organize the data by individuals, departments, school or colleges. If you are working with an existing program, start the data base now and try to get as much past participation data as possible. Do not limit yourself to data on participation but include whatever data satisfy the objectives with which you began the program. It is important to maintain such a database for understanding the effectiveness and dissemination of your efforts. It is appreciated by your faculty, senior administration, and accrediting agencies.

References

Bransford, J. D. (1979). *Human Cognition: Learning, Understanding and Remembering.* Belmont, CA: Wadsworth.

Bruner, J. S. (1964). Course of Cognitive Growth. *American Psychologist, 19*(1), 1-15.

Clark, D., & Redmond, M. (1982). *Small group instructional diagnosis: Final report.* University of Washington, Seattle. FIPSE. ERIC Document Reproduction Service. No. ED 217 954.

Chapter 5

What do the new faculty need to know?

The categories of topics that all faculty need to know about refer to the three principle objectives listed in Chapter 4: the professoriate, instructional development, and serving the institution.

Recall the premise made earlier that the planning of professional development for new faculty is planning for instruction and uses the same planning principles. It should not be surprising then that as regards teaching and learning, the topics that new faculty ought to be familiar with are the same principles of planning for instruction for their students. New faculty need to know that they need to understand the characteristics of their students and need to be able to appraise them so that they can plan their instruction accordingly. Knowing what the demographics of their students are will help faculty relate to them by modifying the level of their language, the pace, the scope, the need for practice, and the effectiveness of different media and methods.

New faculty need to be able to develop objectives and expected outcomes for their students. Just as you the one responsible for professional development of new faculty need to be able to assess whether your new faculty have met the expected outcomes, so do the new faculty need to understand that the preparation of objectives must be congruous with a form of assessment. Objectives and assessments are best prepared when developed simultaneously.

On the basis of the new faculty's appraisal of their students, the new faculty need to be able to select the appropriate equipment, devices, materials that will mediate the experience for the learners in a manner that is appropriate for their students' familiarity with the subject being learned. A practical general rule to follow is Bruner's suggestion for preference of cognitive representation (1964). The more novel a topic is to an individual independent of age, the more appropriate it is to use enactive modes of instruction, that is, hands-on or demonstrative media. As the individual's familiarity increases the iconic presentations—audio and video are effective. When an individual begins to master a topic, symbolic presentations of information are effective. (Refer to Appendix A: Media.)

The appraisal of students' needs to inform the new faculty of how to orchestrate the instructional experience and use the appropriate media. What methods will govern the experience? Refer to Appendix C: Sample Topics for a listing of actual topics used that are categorized by the four areas affecting learning.

Administration of Teaching

The new faculty need to know about the administrative aspects of teaching, institutional policies and procedures, institutional calendars, and administrative offices for grants and research. Following are suggestions some of which are categorized by the factors affecting learning discussed in Chapter 4.

Referring to:

Students
- Their names
- Where to get the class roster
- The purpose of the roster
- How to update the roster: Reporting missing students
- The use of an electronic roster
- Student ID #s
- Still using SS #s?
- The registration process
- Drop add/later registration
- Placement testing: meaning of levels of placement

Media
- Ordering books and other media
- Reserving material at the library
- Electronic reserve of material
- Students' passwords: Is there universal log-in for online material?
- Students' e-mail addresses
- Course management systems such as WebCT, Blackboard, Angel, etc. (learning management systems)
- Who has the responsibility for designing courses…professor or an instructional development (ID) team?
- Who has the responsibility for developing courses…professor or ID team?
- What are the options for teaching at a distance?

- What services are available?
- Who is the contact person?

Instructional Activites: Method
- Is a particular method expected? Cases? Groups? What are the guidelines, protocols, etc.?
- Laboratory, field-site, garage, gymnasium, or other non-classroom facility: scheduling, expectations for use, safety and reporting protocols

Assessment
- Testing calendar
- Electronic testing
- Scoring system: institutional
- Progress reports
- Institutional correspondence concerning progress
- Expectations for frequency and type of assessment
- Testing facilities
- Placement testing: process, interpretation
- Developmental, probationary, etc. students
- Quizes
- Low-stakes versus high-stakes testing

Institutional policies and procedures regarding
- Syllabus preparation
- Student absence
- Grading
- Record keeping

Professor's policies and procedures
- As expressed in the syllabus
- The contractual nature of the syllabus
- The instructional nature of the syllabus

The Academic calendar
- Start dates
- Stop dates
- Drop/add
- Late registration
- Withdrawal
- Pass/fail options
- Holidays
- Test dates
- Professional development dates
- Mid-term grades due dates
- Mid-term warning letters
- Final exam dates
- Final grades due dates

Administration
- Grants office
- Research services office including human subjects review
- Faculty Development office
- Senior administration for academic affairs

What do new faculty need to know about their new academic community?

There is an additional category of information new faculty need to know. It includes the information necessary for making the transition into the institution and community. Depending on the size and resources of your institution, you may consider assigning an individual to coordinating a new faculty transition program or at least devote attention to this area. Although the specifics of what new faculty may need to know may vary by institution, here is a list of topics that are vital to their making a smooth transition to an academic community.

Before They Arrive on Campus

New faculty should be contacted by the facilitator of the development program well before their arrival on campus—ideally, at least one month before their arrival. E-mail and the telephone are preferred because they are the most direct and the fastest.

The first reason for the contact is to begin a relationship between the new faculty member and the Center for Teaching and Learning. The second reason is to identify a contact person for the new faculty member in addition to the department chair, head, or dean whose job it is to help them make a smooth transition to the institution.

What to Discuss During the First Contact

The main purpose of the initial contact is to inform the faculty member of the services the Center can provide for them and to answer questions they might have about the transition process. In addition, it is to provide them with information about making a transition. Individual faculty should be sent a packet of information designed to help them with everything from preparing a course syllabus to finding a place of worship, a day care center or dentist. Another purpose is to reinforce that the new professor can contact the Center anytime with any kind of question and that help will be there for them.

What is in the packet of information sent to new faculty?

Academically Related Information

The contents of a packet will depend on the individual institution but the following list represents what new faculty at Ferris State have indicated over the past five years were of great value to them.

1. A completed model of a well written course syllabus (on disk) that can be used to help faculty develop their syllabi.

2. A blank course syllabus template–on disk or online– that faculty can use to build their course syllabi.

3. A calendar of events for the week faculty report for work. To include any Human Resource department orientation meetings, Department, School or College meeting times and days, all other required or voluntarly orientation activities for new faculty.

4. A schedule of pay days for the semester—especially when the first pay check will be received.

5. A semester calendar showing class starting and completion dates, all holidays or breaks, final exam week and the date grades are due. You may want to include a copy of the calendar of the local schools as well.

6. A statement of when and where faculty can locate their student class lists.

7. A list of the passwords, IDs, and access codes that each person will need to use the various electronic information systems on campus and from whom or where they can obtain these codes. We found that this was vital to new faculty as they tried to prepare for their classes and research activities. It was also one of their greatest frustrations when they were unable to access e-mail or phone mail or various computer information systems. Including a brief explana-

tion of how the e-mail and phone systems (how to get an outside line or call long distance) work is also a good idea.

8. Information as to where and from whom they can get keys to their buildings, labs and offices.

9. A statement of where and when they can get a parking pass and the cost of parking.

10. A brief description of what course management system (Blackboard, WebCT, Angel etc.) the campus uses and a contact person for questions about using the system.

11. The name of a contact person to assist in taking advantage of educational benefits for themselves, their spouses or children. Many colleges and universities offer tuition discounts for family members but the paper work to take advantage of it needs to be processed well in advance of the date of the beginning of classes.

Personal Transition Assistance

Include these items:

1. A packet of information prepared by the Chamber of Commerce about the businesses and services available to new members of the community. Make certain there is information about realtors that handle both sales and rentals.

2. Information about the local schools—include listing of public, private and charter schools, and pre-schools in the immediate area and a contact person for each.

3. Information about the availability of on- or off-campus short-term housing for faculty. Many of the faculty in our program have listed this as a high priority

for them and one the most valuable services that helped make their transition easier.

4. Specific information about day care services in the immediate area of campus. (This may or may not be part of the Chamber of Commerce information.) This has been listed as a high priority by faculty.
5. A listing of the website of the local city or town, if available.

In summary, the new faculty need to know about planning for instruction as well as how to make the transition into their new lives.

References

Bruner, J. S. (1964). Vourse of cognitive growth. *American Psychologist, 19*(1), 1-15.

Chapter 6

What to do on the first day of a new faculty program

The emphasis will be on making the professional, social, and cultural transition. The first face-to-face meeting between the facilitator and the new faculty is an exciting and important day for the success of the program. Although new faculty are extremely busy during the week before classes begin, it is vital that they meet as a group to begin the orientation process to their new academic community and city or town.

Enough Time

The week before classes is always a tremendously busy period. Plan your opening session to range from 3–6 hours to allow enough time for both the relationship building portion of the program as well as to notify the incoming faculty of the most urgent information concerning their professional responsibilities and the beginning of classes. If there is a large group of new faculty, break it up into smaller groups then conduct this initial session more than once; or, offer it by schools or colleges so that they can attend in smaller groups. The dynamics of working with large groups of students applies in working with large groups of faculty. Creating a sense of intimacy by acknowledging individuals is challenging and sometimes not possible if the group is too large.

What to Do First

Because of the belief that learning is greatly enhanced when those involved feel a sense of connection or relationship with the teacher and each other (Weimer, 2002; Bransford 1999; Rogers, 1999) step one of the transition emphasis is devoted to initiating connections among the individual members of the new faculty themselves as well as with the program facilitator. This activity can be conducted in a variety of ways, however choosing a method that is enjoyable and reveals both professional and personal information about the new faculty is a key to making this time valuable.

There are two goals for this initial step in the transition program. First, the new faculty need to feel comfortable with the facilitator and be willing to ask questions and participate fully in the day's activities. Second, the new faculty need to get to know each other and learn what they have in common professionally and personally. New faculty have found colleagues that were deeply involved in similar research interests, hobbies, scouting and sports. They also discovered people who studied or worked at colleges or universities where they had worked or studied. Most importantly, the faculty felt less isolated and began to develop a sense of collegiality with the members of their new academic community.

What Activities Promote Connection?

Many activities could be used to bring about faculty interaction but the ones described below have been used with great success. The first activity is to begin with a routing process of asking each member to formally introduce him or herself relating individual professional background, teaching or research interest, former professional experience, academic degrees, and a little about one's family and personal interests. Giving the faculty a specific list of information to share is helpful as it keeps the playing field level and promotes comfort during this initial interaction. It has been our experience that meetings, workshops, classes etc. often limit the relationship-building to this one–time activity. This is clearly not enough interaction. For the program to be a success faculty need to develop a sense of community over an extended period of time. If you limit the introductions to a formal style, the tone will be a formal one. New faculty need more than just formal interaction to begin feeling comfortable with the new environment. To accomplish this, one or two of the following ice breaker activities are suggested. These activities are specifically designed to allow personal interaction as well as helping to reveal additional information about the group's members.

1. Human Treasure Hunt—this exercise not only requires the participants to get up on their feet and meet and greet each other but it can also be written in a way so that it reveals any of a wide variety of information about the audience. The rules are simple. Each person is handed a sheet of paper with 15 questions related to the hobbies and personal

experiences of the group. Their job is to find at least two people that have these hobbies or have done the activities listed on the form by meeting each person in the group and asking them about the items listed. An example would be, "Have you taught outside the United States?" or, "Have you traveled to China?" or, "Do you play golf?" The activity takes about 15 minutes to complete. When all the questions are answered then each item on the list is read aloud and all who have answered, "Yes" to the question are acknowledged. In this way, the new faculty discover additional connections between themselves and others in the group.

2. Tissue paper—this rather resourceful use of bathroom tissue paper is a fun activity that creates interest and reveals additional information about the group for all to hear. The activity is simple. A role of common bathroom tissue paper is handed to the person sitting closest to the facilitator with the single statement, "Take what you need." The roll is passed along and each person takes what he or she needs. When the last member of the group has taken a portion of the tissue the facilitator asks each member of the group to tell the group something about him or herself for each sheet of tissue they had taken—one sheet, one statement— 20 sheets twenty statements. The activity takes 10–15 minutes to complete and again reveals additional information about the new faculty members. Facilitators take note! If someone has taken 20–25 sheets you may have to help by asking questions—some people have trouble telling 20 things about themselves.

3. Interview a Partner—Similarities and Differences. This activity allows two people in the group to get to know each other on a more personal level. Each member of

the group is assigned a partner. Partners are to work together to find 10 things about themselves that are similar and 10 things that are different. Suggestions are given for the types of things to think about like food, music, sports, movies, family etc. This activity takes about 10 minutes. Once completed, one member of the pair shares the similarities that were discovered and the other shares the difference with whole group. This sharing works to reveal additional information about the group that may allow for further connections to be made.

Other "Day One" Activities

Another focus of a first meeting with new faculty may include taking care of urgent business. Consider dealing with such issues as employment questions, the start of classes, rules and policies of the institution, passwords and access codes, the demographic profile of the student population, and academic expectations (tenure and promotion).

A good starting point for covering these issues is a presentation on the demographics of the student population. Even at institutions that are highly selective and one would expect the students to be predictably homogenous, faculty enjoy and benefit from being informed about the characteristics of the student body. At institutions that are highly selective or that practice open admission, there is likely more variety among the students. The new faculty who most often seem prepared for the variety of the student body are those who have taught at similar institutions. Faculty who are newly out of graduate school, who have not taught, or have taught at selective institutions are typically very surprised when they meet a diverse student body because their expectations are challenged. They will need to adjust their teaching approaches to meet the needs of their students as a result. An example of a common response is for new faculty to expect that their new students will be able to work at the pace, level, and capacity of the new professor. For this reason, it is imperative that the faculty be briefed not only on the student demographics but also on the kind of learning behaviors that they can expect in the classroom.

An excellent follow up to this presentation is a panel presentation and discussion conducted of current teaching faculty about their experiences in teaching at the institution. Faculty learn well from each other. Over the years, our new faculty have attested to the benefits they enjoyed from such panel discussions about the student population, the challenges encountered and the sharing of teaching tips that have worked especially well for them. Schedule the panel presentation to be followed by a question and answer period and, best of all, schedule it so it ends at lunch time and include panel members for lunch to continue talking informally with the new faculty.

A useful activity for the first day session is to review the writing of a well-designed syllabus. Some institutions provide sample syllabi for their faculty to use as models as a part of the initial contact with new faculty. Even if this is the case at your institution, it is recommended that some time be given to syllabus preparation during the initial meeting with the incoming faculty. Writing a syllabus may not be an entirely new activity for all of the incoming faculty, but for others it will be completely new process. Others again may have written syllabi, but were not instructed on the critical elements of a syllabus and of its nature as a legal document.

Two additional activities that are of great value to new faculty during the first day session are a discussion of admission and enrollment practices during the first week of classes and a discussion of effective ways to begin a course that can help establish a positive learning environment. Institutions have their own ways of conducting dropping and adding of classes and late admission of students. New faculty need to know about adjusting rosters based on dropping and adding, actions to take when students appear on class lists but are not appearing in class—or the opposite—students who are in class but not on the class roster. For example, some students may have been dropped for non-payment but may not be aware of it. It is also helpful to discuss any specific academic policies concerning student academic misconduct, about having an attendance policy, requiring activities outside of class time, informing about regulations for class field trips, and any other policies relating to student behavior, enrollment, or admissions.

The second activity is a brief discussion of teaching and learning with a focus on what faculty can do in the first few meetings with students to establish a positive learning environment, to begin the process of creating connections and relationships with students and to establish a clear understanding of the role students will play in their own learning during the semester. Suggestions include:

1. Include a sample of Ice Breakers that can be used with students to begin the process of building community.
2. Give faculty ideas on how to quickly learn their students' names.

For example:

Take a photo of each student (with permission) and write the student's name on the back of the photo. Students find this to be fun and appreciate the genuine interest the instructor is showing in getting to know them.

Play the name game. This can be done with groups of thirty or less. The game begins with the first student telling his or her first name and a word to describe him or herself—the more interesting or different the word, the better. Each subsequent student must repeat all of the names and identify words for every student that has come before him or her. This sounds difficult but the repetition of the names and words along with the visual cues of the faces makes it fairly easy to do. By the time the last person has tried to repeat all of the names and identifying words, both the students and instructor will know most of the names of everyone in the class.

Use a seating chart—a simple but effective way to learn names! Once student have chosen seats in a class, they tend to sit in them for the entire semester. For that reason, you can reliably use a seating chart.

Have students wear name tags the first few classes. This is inexpensive and works well to establish communication between the professor and the students. The name tag can also include the name of the student's hometown and can help to promote further connection among students who may live near the same place.

3. Discuss with new faculty that they need to make themselves available to students from the very first

day of class. Suggest that faculty invite students to visit them during their office hours or at other times that they are available. A sincere and repeated invitation to students to visit is a sign that the instructor really does want to build community in the classroom.

References

Bransford, J. D., Brown, A. L., & Cocking, R. R. (1999). *How people learn: Brain, mind, experience, and school.* Washington, DC: National Academy Press. [Available online at http://www.nap.edu/html/howpeople1/].

Rogers, S. (1999). *Motivation & learning, the high performance toolbox and teaching tips.* Evergreen, Colorado: Peak Learning Systems.

Weimer, M. (2002). *Learner-centered teaching 2002.* San Francisco: Jossey-Bass.

New Faculty Professional Development

Chapter 7

Logistics

The topics in this book were written to cover the essentials necessary for an ideal program. There are a number of logistics that need to be considered. To assist your planning, specifications are suggested. While the premise of this planning guide is the ideal program under ideal conditions, the expectation is that an actual professional development program for new faculty will not comprise the entire set of ideal conditions and logistics but still will function successfully. What you need to do is to identify the needs of a program that are of highest priority for your institution and then focus on the conditions and logistics that would support your program.

Database

Begin a database for all the activities in which your new faculty participate. Record participation rates for individuals, programs, departments, schools, or colleges. You should be doing this already for your current faculty. Keep data for the new faculty as well and compare rates over the years. Collect anecdotal information as well. This is valuable information for your planning, for budgeting, for senior administration, and for accrediting agencies.

Scheduling

A somewhat self-contradicting double goal is for new faculty to meet often enough so that they feel a part of the program yet they do not meet so often that they are overwhelmed or threatened and start to resent the program. Schedules should not interfere with other job requirements, such as department, school, college, or committee meetings. Many institutions keep open times during a month or semester especially for professional development activities. Ideally, new faculty would meet bi-weekly and meetings last for one and a half hours.

Faculty should visit the classes of 3 other professors—One from their area, two from other areas. One of the benefits of this practice is the observation of what actually occurs in college instruction. It is also an opportunity to take away ideas for teaching. It should also result in the two professors at least making each other's acquaintance as well.

Personnel

One way to look at staffing your professional development program for new faculty is first to consider categories of job functions, then to estimate what parts of those functions can be assumed by individuals. This is in contrast to first identifying the individuals and assigning functions to them. Three main categories are coordination, facilitation, and clerical.

Coordination

This category in general terms is responsible for organizing the events to be conducted. The specific activities include identifying the topics to be taught, creating schedules, meeting with new faculty, meeting with senior administration, meeting with deans, meeting with facilitators, and clerical staff, and being a spokesperson for the program.

Clerical

This category in general terms includes putting into effect many of the plans of the coordinators and facilitators. The activities include communicating with faculty—e-mail, surface mail, telephone—identifying meeting places, scheduling events, ordering supplies, equipment, and food. This category also includes creating and maintaining the database recording participation in activities—a performance database. There needs to be communication with coordinators and facilitators as well.

Facilitation

This category in general terms includes the teaching activities the specifics of which are planning the lessons, planning the program, preparing for the sessions, conducting the lessons, assessing learning, collecting feedback on the lessons, getting feedback from new faculty and responding to them about it as well as communicating about the feedback to coordinators and clerical staff.

Compensation—Faculty Work Schedules

There does not need to be extra remuneration to new faculty for participation in a professional development program. There should, however, be accommodations in scheduling their teaching in three critical dimensions: new faculty should have a minimal number of different class preparations, new faculty should be assigned a minimal number of advisees and advising should be done with the mentorship of a department colleague. Finally, new faculty should be assigned a minimal number of classes for which they must first study in order to be able to teach. The guiding principal is to schedule the work so that new faculty can progress in the quantity and complexity of the work they are assigned. Overloading new faculty can lead to burnout and reduce the value they can bring to their students and their research.

Facilities

There should be a readily available facility designated for faculty professional development. It would be equipped with media: books, videos, journals, etc. about teaching and learning. It would include a food-serving, but not food-preparation, kitchen. The area would have space for large group meetings as well as quiet study and small group meeting areas.

Equipment

There need to be computers for training and the related equipment: projectors, display surfaces such as electronic white boards, etc. that are normally used to facilitate teaching and learning.

Communication

There should be a system for the managers of the professional development program to communicate with the new faculty. There should be a system for the new faculty to communicate with each other as a group that may be the aforementioned system or a different one such as a listserv, e-mail group address, or a discussion board.

Senior administration should communicate with new faculty directly for the purpose of introduction.

Professional Development Facilities

There should be institutional office spaces for the director and for the staff that meet the institutional standards for accommodation, equipment, and furniture.

Food and refreshments

Meals or refreshments are provided as appropriate to the time of day and the length of the session.

Educational Travel

Groups of new faculty can be given opportunities to travel to national professional conferences which can serve as a reward for participation and are excellent teaching development activities.

Part of the program schedule may include an all-expenses paid participation in an educational conference to occur within the first year. (This is part of the Ferris program.) Notice that the suggestion is for an educational conference and not one in a professor's subject area. Remember the goal is to learn about teaching and learning. It would be best, too if groups of the new faculty participated together. Some conferences to consider include those conducted by the International Alliance of Teacher Scholars (www.iats.com). They are offered regionally and focus on teaching and learning practices. Other conference venues include the Professional and Organizational network (POD), American Association for Higher Education (AAHE), American Association of Colleges and Universities

(AACU), and the Association for Educational Communications and Technology (AECT), etc.

Mentors

A trained, capable, and willing mentor should be assigned to work with the new faculty member; however, the new faculty transition program may also serve a mentoring function.

Costs

Personnel: At a minimum, the salary of the managing administrator, the director, and the clerical staff ought to be a part of the general funding. It is practical to grant faculty release time to work with the professional development program. The cost of their release is the amount needed to replace them for their term of service. A concern with faculty on release time is the impracticality of dedicating faculty for large percentages of release time for long periods. On the one hand, a long term assignment promotes consistency and stability, on the other, rotating the membership of faculty on release time promotes the professional development of a larger number of extant faculty.

Stipends: There does not need to be a stipend to new faculty participating in a professional development program conducted on their behalf.

These are cost areas to consider:
• Food and refreshments:
• Honoraria for speakers
• Materials

- Supplies
- Travel

Use this listing of logistic considerations in planning your professional development program for new faculty. It is likely that you will encounter considerations that have not been foreseen. Keep records of them.

Afterword — What's next?

After the first yearlong new faculty program at Ferris, we continued working with the "graduating class." That is, we began calling meetings of faculty during their second, third, etc. years at the institution. The faculty also participated in the professional development activities for all current faculty, but their special status was acknowledged. It did not take much to do other than to have a meeting with an activity such as a topical panel. We would even combine cohort groups of prevoiusly new faculty to have large meetings. It contributed to the sense of participation and camaraderie and we think had a significant effect on the desire of faculty to remain at the institution.

It would be useful to develop a model of "developmental progression" of a faculty career. It would include types of knowledge about teaching and learning that a professor would learn over the years. For example, the expectations for a professor with five years of experience ought to be different than one with fifteen years of experience, as long as the operational term is "progressive." Such a model would be valuable to planning long term activities as well as activities for professors in a developmental range. This is a consideration for the future.

Appendices

Appendix A

Examples of Media

Examples of Traditional Media Used

a. Projected Static visuals: opaque projection, over-head projection, slides, filmstrips

b. Non-projected Static visuals: pictures, photographs, charts, graphs, diagrams, displays, exhibits, bulletin boards

c. Audio: records, tapes, CDs

d. Multimedia Presentations: sound slides

e. Print: Text books, workbooks, job aids

f. Dynamic Projected Visuals: Film, videotape, television

g. Games, simulation games, puzzles

h. Realia: Models, manipulatives, specimens, industrial equipment

i. Laboratories: clinics, garages, kitchens, etc.

j. Humans: voice and demonstrations with body

Examples of New Technology Media Used

a. Web-based: faculty presence, web-enabled complements, web-based courses, course management systems or learning management systems: WebCT, BlackBoard

b. Computer-assisted instruction

c. Teleconferences

d. Webcasts

e. Electronic mail: threaded discussions, individual mail, group distributions
f. Flowcharting programs: concept-mapping software (Inspiration, SemNet)
g. Digital Video Disc (DVD)
h. 2-way interactive TV
i. hybrid-instruction: web-based, web-enhanced instruction

Adapted from Seels, B. & Glasgow, Z. (1990) *Exercises in Instructional Design*: Merrill.

Appendix B

Examples of Methods

Methods (instructional strategies)
a. Discovery Learning
b. Reception Learning
c. Lecture
d. Laboratory: clinic, garage, kitchen, etc.
e. Internship: field-based
f. Discussion
g. Readings
h. Field trips
i. Note-taking
j. Demonstrations
k. Programmed instruction: linear or branching
l. Drill and practice
m. Tutorial
n. Role play
o. Exercises
p. Independent study
q. Simulations
r. Problem-based learning
s. Case study
t. Lecture
u. Reading

Adapted from Seels, B. & Glasgow, Z. (1990) *Exercises in Instructional Design*: Merrill.

Appendix C

Sample Topics

What do faculty members need to know about? Following are titles of actual professional development sessions used at Pennsylvania College of Technology or Ferris State University. The titles were categorized using the model of "Factors affecting learning" (Bransford, 1979): learners' characteristics, and instructional activities, media assessment as well as the areas of administrative responsibilities and advising. Some titles refer to more than one area.

Learner Characteristics
a. Effective Teaching Relies on Understanding How People Learn
b. Matching Students Learning Styles to Teaching Styles
c. Integrating "Learning How to Learn" (Study Strategies) into Your Content Teaching
d. Adapting to the Varied Characteristics of you Students: Gender, Ethnicity, and Age
e. Motivating Students to be More Active Learners
f. Methods and Learners
g. Art of Confrontation
h. Dealing with Classroom Disruptions—Why Students Disrupt Class and How to Deal with Disruptive Students

i. Effective Advising Begins with Understanding the Characteristics of Today's College Students
j. Maintaining Professional Teacher/Student Relationships with your Students
k. Communicating with Students Outside of Class
l. Techniques for Remembering Students' Names
m. Community in the Classroom
n. Study Skills for All Majors
o. Study Skills for Math, Science & Technology
p. Dealing with Difficult Students
q. Now What Do I Do? Dealing with Uncivil Behaviors in the Classroom
r. Institutional: Classroom Violence: What Can I Do?
s. Institutional: Who is the Person with the Disability?

Instructional Activities
a. Writing a Syllabus
b. If You Are Going to Lecture, Do It Well
c. How to Ask Questions
d. Getting Students to Interact: Tools for Discussion. Inject Vitality into Teaching (Get Excited!)
e. I'm Hip to Your Vibe, Groove Merchant (Music & Learning)
f. Integrating Critical Thinking Skills into Your Content Teaching
g. Instructional Methods that Address Learners Varied Characteristics
h. How Not to Be Professor Boring: How to Get Your Students Active in Class
i. Using Case Studies in Your Instruction
j. The West Point Method for Presenting and Pacing Instruction

k. Tips From Toastmasters: Watch the Classroom Come Alive
l. Dick Jones is a Brand Name (A Unique Method of Teaching)
m. Learning, the Learner and Teaching Methodology: A Survey of Educational Practice
n. Applications of Teaching Methods: In-depth Exploration of Core Teaching Methods
o. Let's Open a Bag of Theatrical Tricks for Teaching
p. Comedy in College: Laugh Your Way to Learning
q. Insider Tips on Easy Ways to Improve Student Writing
r. Broken Squares: An Exercise in Building Cooperation in the Classroom and in Life
s. Lecturing can be an Active Learning Process
t. Critical Thinking
u. Collaborative Learning - Working in Groups
v. Spicing up Dry Lectures
w. Information Literacy Illustrated
x. Study Skills: Help Your Students Succeed
y. Update on Cooperative Education
z. Teaching: Planning Teaching & Learning
aa. Technology: Accessing Resources on the Campus Network

Assessment
a. Writing Effective Tests
b. Use of Informal Classroom Assessment Techniques
c. Feedback and Program Evaluation Session
d. Student Assessment Techniques
e. Writing Great Multiple Choice Test Questions
f. Finding Out if Your Student Are Learning
g. Ten Tips to Make You a Better Test Writer
h. Testing: What is it?

i.   Panel Discussion: Alternative Testing Techniques

j.   Examining Assessment from Both Sides of the Desk

Media

a.   The Excel A&P Gradebook

b.   Technology in the Classroom

c.   HorizonLive—Creating On-demand Instruction

d.   Technology in the Classroom—Hybridization of Computer-based Instruction with Traditional In-class Teaching

e.   WebCT Summer Institute

f.   On-line Grade Submission

g.   Using On-Line Discussion Boards

h.   Communicating with Your Students Using GroupWise E-Mail

i.   Orientation to the Technology-Enhanced Classroom

j.   Introduction to Web Supplementation

k.   Accessing Resources on the Campus Network

l.   Pros & Cons of Web Supplementation

m.   Introduction to WebCT 4.1

n.   Upgrading to WebCT 4.

o.   Pixels Not Paper: Another Crossroad on the Digital Highway

p.   Using Webcasts

Administration

a.   Sexual Harassment Prevention Workshop for Faculty

b.   The Penn College Library: What Faculty Really Need to Know

c.   Video Presentation of "First Day" – Planning your Syllabus

d.   Feeling a Part of the Institution

e. Academic Policies that Affect Advising—Do you know them
f. Understanding the Current Mathematics Placement Process
g. Alcohol Problems on Campus: Resources for the Classroom Teacher

Bransford, J. D. (1979). *Human Cognition: Learning, Understanding and Remembering.* Belmont, CA: Wadsworth.

List of References

Atkinson, R.C., & Shiffrin, R.M. (1968). Human memory: A proposed system and its control processes. In K. W. Spence & J. T. Spence (Eds.), *Psychology of learning and motivation* (Vol. 2). New York: Academic Press.

Ausubel, D.P. (1968). *Educational psychology, A cognitive view.* New York: Holt, Rinehart and Winston.

Boorstin, D.J. (1995). *Cleopatra's nose: Essays on the unexpected.* New York: Vintage.

Bransford, J. D. (1979). *Human Cognition: Learning, Understanding and Remembering.* Belmont, CA: Wadsworth.

Bransford, J. D., Brown, A. L., & Cocking, R. R. (1999). *How people learn: Brain, mind, experience, and school.* Washington, DC: National Academy Press. pp.xi [Available online at http://www.nap.edu/html/howpeople1/].

Bruner, J. S. (1964). Course of Cognitive Growth. *American Psychologist, 19*(1), 1-15.

Clark, D., & Redmond, M. (1982). *Small group instructional diagnosis: Final report.* University of Washington, Seattle. FIPSE. ERIC Document Reproduction Service. No. ED 217 954.

Doyle, T. (2003) *Summary of the first five years of the New to Ferris Faculty Transition Program.* Big Rapids, MI: Ferris State University.

Gilbert, T. F. (1978). *Human competence: Engineering worthy performance.* New York: McGraw Book Company.

Goldberg, E. (2001). *The executive brain, frontal lobes and the civilized mind.* New York: Oxford University Press.

Keller, J. M. (1987). Development and use of the ARCS model of motivational design. *Journal of Instructional Development, 10*(3), 2-10.

Kossyln, A. (1996). *Images and the brain.* Cambridge, MA: MIT Press.

Kuh, G. D., Schuh, J.S., Whitt, E.J., & Associates (1991). *Involving colleges: Successful approaches to fostering student learning and personal development outside the classroom.* San Francisco: Jossey-Bass.

LeDoux, J. (2001). *The emotional brain.* New York: Simon & Schuster.

Levine, A. & Cureton, J.S. (1999). *When hope and fear collide: A portrait of today's college student.* San Francisco: Jossey-Bass.

Marcinkiewicz, H. R., Regstad, N. G. (1996). Using subjective norms to predict teachers' computer use. *Journal of Computing in Teacher Education, 13*(1), 27–33

Marcinkiewicz, H. R., & Sylwester, R. (November/December, 2003). The brain, technology, and education: An interview with Robert Sylwester. The Technology Source [http://ts.mivu.org]

Teaching Ideas #8: Essential demographics of today's college students. (November, 1998). *AAHE-Bulletin, 51*(3).

Sylwester, R. (1995) *A celebration of neurons: An educator's guide to the human brain.* Chicago: Zephyr Press.

Starbuck, W.H. (1996). Unlearning ineffective or obsolete technologies. *International Journal of Technology Management, 11*, 725-737.

Rogers, S. (1999). *Motivation & learning, the high performance toolbox and teaching tips.* Evergreen, Colorado: Peak Learning Systems.

Simon, H. (1996). Observations on the sciences of science learning. Paper presented at Carnegie Mellon University.

Senge, P. (1990). *The fifth discipline.* New York: Currency
    Doubleday

Seldin, P. & Associates, (1995). *Improving college teaching.*
    Bolton, MA: Anker.

Rogers, S. (1999). *Motivation & learning, the high performance
    toolbox and teaching tips.* Evergreen, Colorado: Peak Learn-
    ing Systems.

Weimer, M. (2002). *Learner-centered teaching 2002.* San Fran-
    cisco: Jossey-Bass.

Zull, J. (2002). *The art of changing the brain.* Sterling, VA: Stylus